Rhino is one of the largest living mammal in the World

There are 5 species
of Rhino in the World

There are two African rhino species white & black rhinos

Asian Rhino species includes Greater one horned, Sumatran and Javan rhinos

The word rhinoceros is a literal mix of two Greek words : rhino (nose) and ceros (horn)

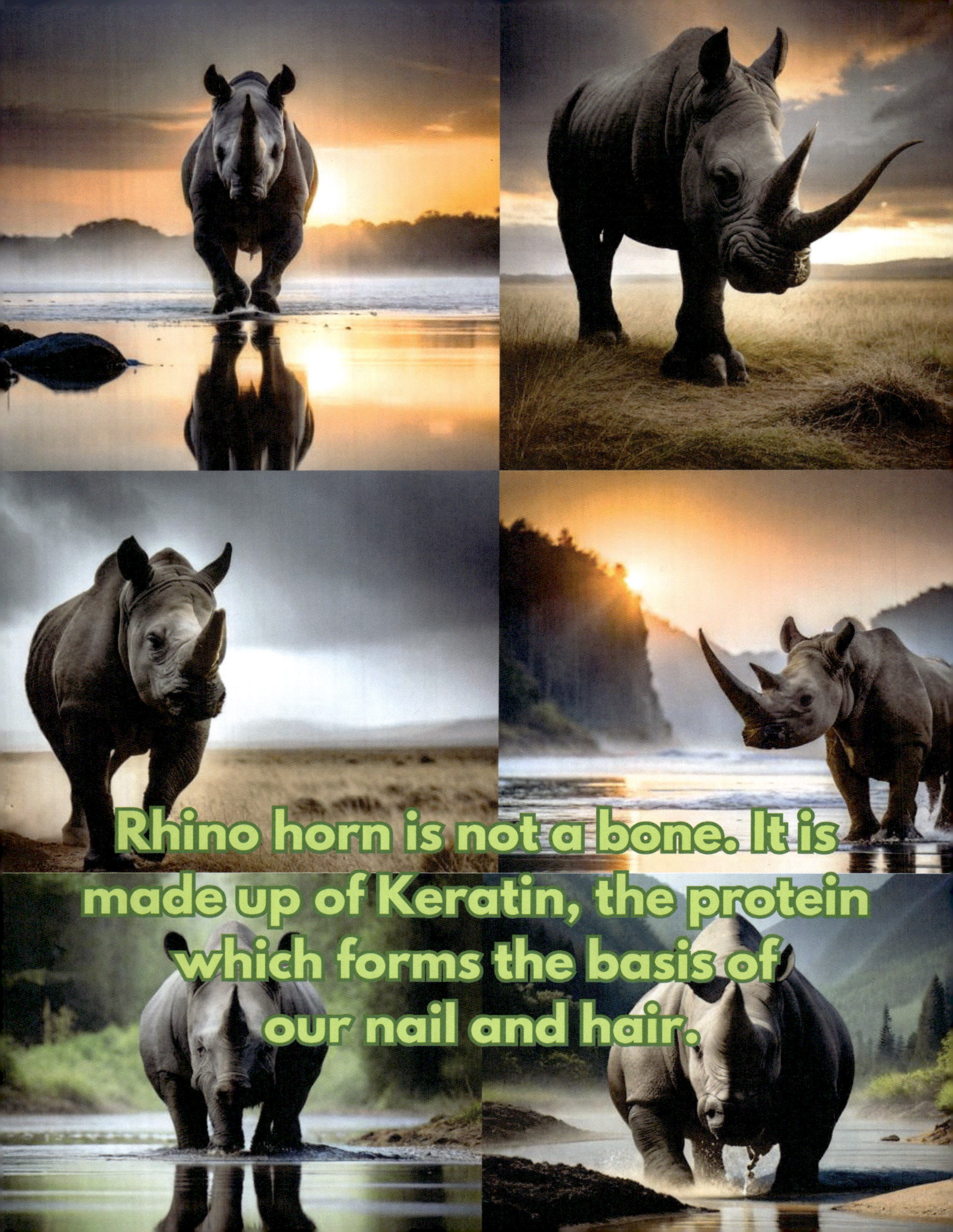

Rhino horn is not a bone. It is made up of Keratin, the protein which forms the basis of our nail and hair.

One horn rhino and Javan rhino have one horn whereas rest three species have two horns.

Rhinos can weigh up to 3500 kilograms. White rhinoceros are the third largest land mammal after the African and Asian elephants

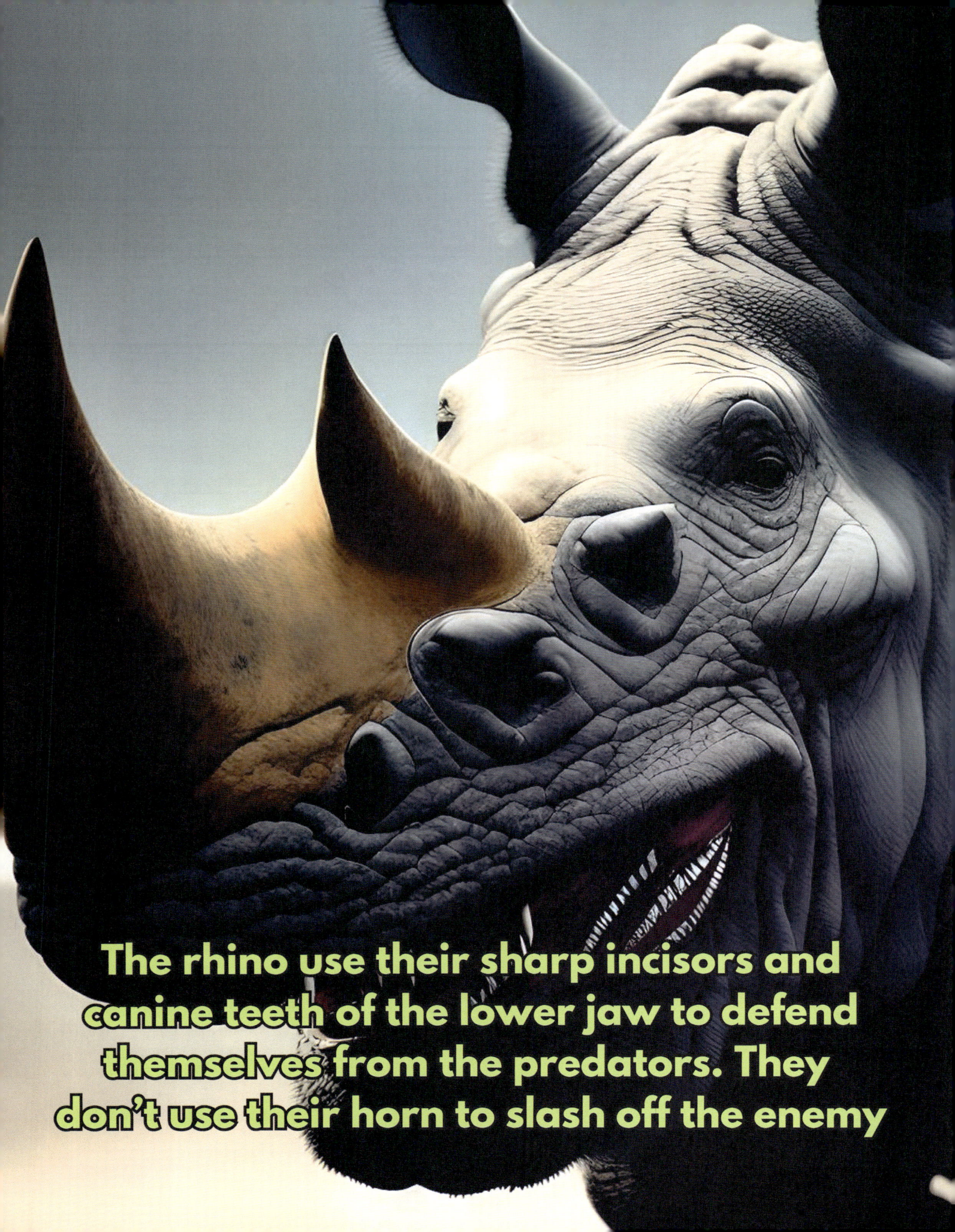

The rhino use their sharp incisors and canine teeth of the lower jaw to defend themselves from the predators. They don't use their horn to slash off the enemy

Rhinos are blessed with sharp hearing and smelling sense, thus they can get you by your odor

Rhinos have poor vision. They're unable to see a motionless person at a distance of 30 meter.

Don't go on the size, they are very fast

Rhinos can run at a speed of 30 -40 miles per hour. Figures say that the speed of an Olympic runner is around 15 miles per hour. Thus, a rhino can outrun a human!

Rhinos love to live with their extended families groups.

Rhinos feed mostly in the cool of the early morning, during the late afternoon, or at night.

Indian rhinos are herbivores. They eat grass, leaves, fruit, branches and aquatic plants, as well as cultivated crops. They drink daily and are fond of mineral licks.

During the day, they spend a lot of time in the water or wallowing in the mud in order to keep cool

Rhinos are excellent swimmer

Rhinos are known to make about 10 sounds, including snorts, honks, and roars.

An adult rhino's skin may be as thick as 5 cm (2 inches). It's protective skin formed from layers of <u>collagen</u> positioned in a <u>lattice</u> structure.

Rhinos communicate through honks, sneezes...and poo.

They can smell the poo and urine of other individuals, and know who's in the area.

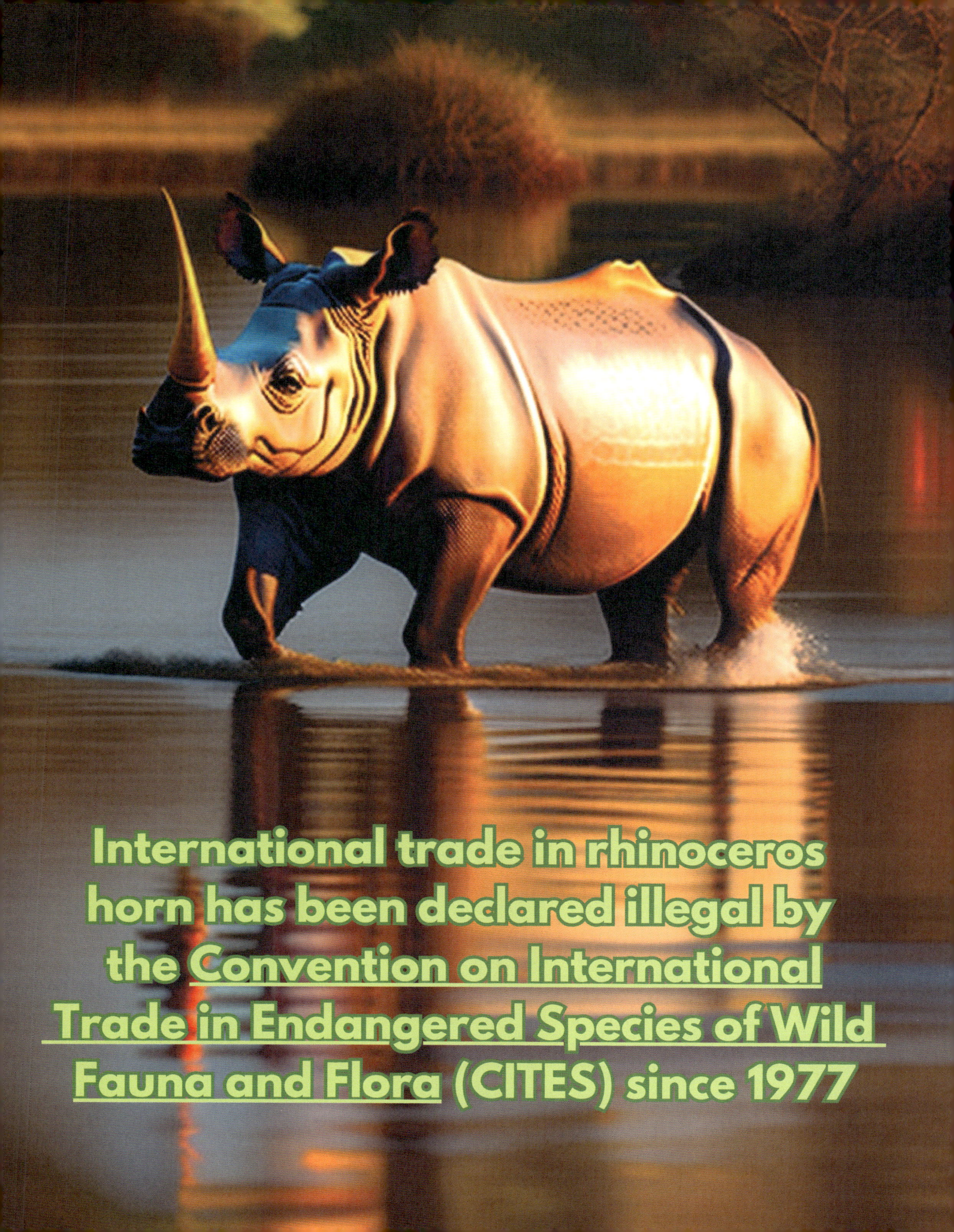

International trade in rhinoceros horn has been declared illegal by the Convention on International Trade in Endangered Species of Wild Fauna and Flora (CITES) since 1977

In the early 20th century, there were about 500,000 rhinos in Asia and Africa, according to the World Wildlife Fund. However, by 1970, rhino numbers dropped to 70,000, and today, around 27,000 rhinos remain in the wild.

Out of 4000 individuals of the Greater Indian Rhinoceros population, nearly 85% is concentrated in Assam, where Kaziranga National Park contains 70% of the rhino population.

In a report published in 2022, there are 22,137 rhinos in Africa, of which 6,195 black rhinos and 15,942 white rhinos.

World Rhino Day is celebrated on 22nd September every day

Printed in Great Britain
by Amazon